Beamingly Brilliant Bears

David R Morgan

illustrated by Anastasia Kotelnikova

A2Z
PRESS

Beamingly Brilliant Bears

This is a work of fiction.

Text and Illustrations copyrighted

by David R Morgan ©2023

Library of Congress Control Number: 2022920351

Printed in the United States of America

A 2 Z Press LLC

PO Box 582

Deleon Springs, FL 32130

bestlittleonlinebookstore.com

sizemore3630@aol.com

440-241-3126

ISBN: 978-1-954191-81-5

Dedication

To Bex and Toby
who are brilliantly
*beyond **bear**able*
and
to Sue, who
***bears** with me*

This Book Belongs To:

_____

Beamingly brilliant bears love honey made by bees,
And they enjoy napping under trees.
Bears come in all shapes and sizes,
Read this book – it's filled with all sorts of surprises!

Bears can be cuddly or very big and mean.
The cuddly ones are like my Teddy Bear,
the cutest I've seen.

Yes, my friendly Teddy is the truest friend,
He's a little bear I can pick up by either end.

Teddy's shiny fur is the colour of honey on toast,
He's a forever friend that will never boast.

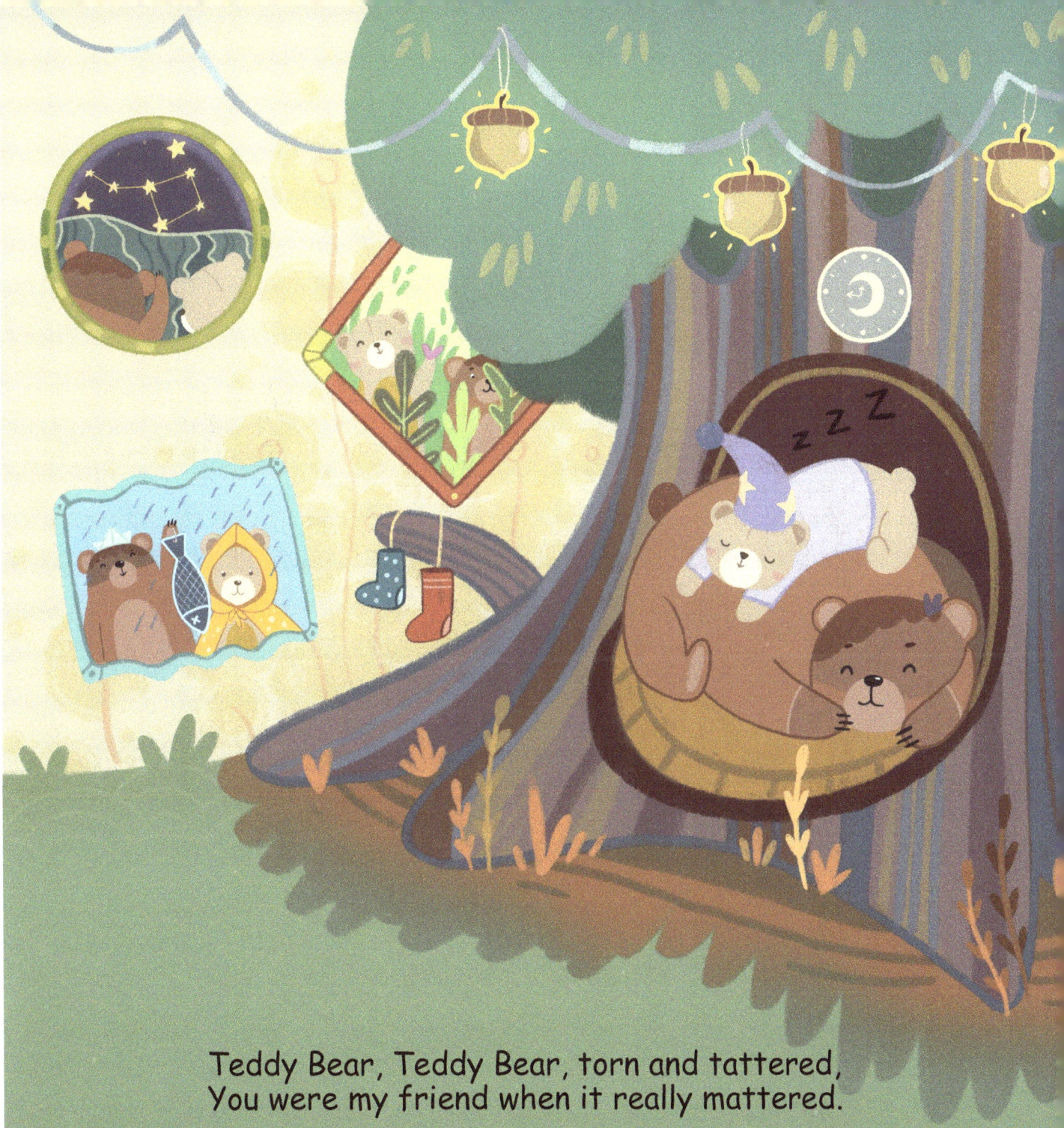

Teddy Bear, Teddy Bear, torn and tattered,
You were my friend when it really mattered.

There are many, not just one type of bear
in our world, so let's see which of them is where.

BEARS
around the world

AMERICAN BLACK

GIANT PANDA

SIRIAN BROWN

KODIAK

Let's mention that Bears have many layers of soft hair,
They have very sharp claws and tails that are barely there.

Tail

The BEAR Times

Also cuddly and cute, are fluffy koala bears that
eat eucalyptus leaves, come see,
The koalas' mommies have a pouch like the possum and wallaby.

And, like other marsupials, she keeps her
baby in her pouch there,
But bears don't have pouches which
means the koala is not a true bear!

KOALA

NOT A BEAR

Do you recall that silly story, where
three bears get the blame?
Yes, the one with that girl -
Goldilocks was her name,

GOLDILOCKS

The story of her eating, sleeping and breaking a chair!
It's really so unfair and unreasonable for any bear!

EATING

SLEEPING

BREAKING

A CHAIR

The little girl was wakened with an ear-piercing shriek,
Facing three hairy bears, she was unable to speak.

But, it wasn't polite to sneak into their home,
Bears should be left to live peacefully alone.

BEARS want to live PEACEFULLY alone

The Moral

Time to learn - a family or group of bears is called a "sleuth,"
And their sense of smell is the best, that's the truth!

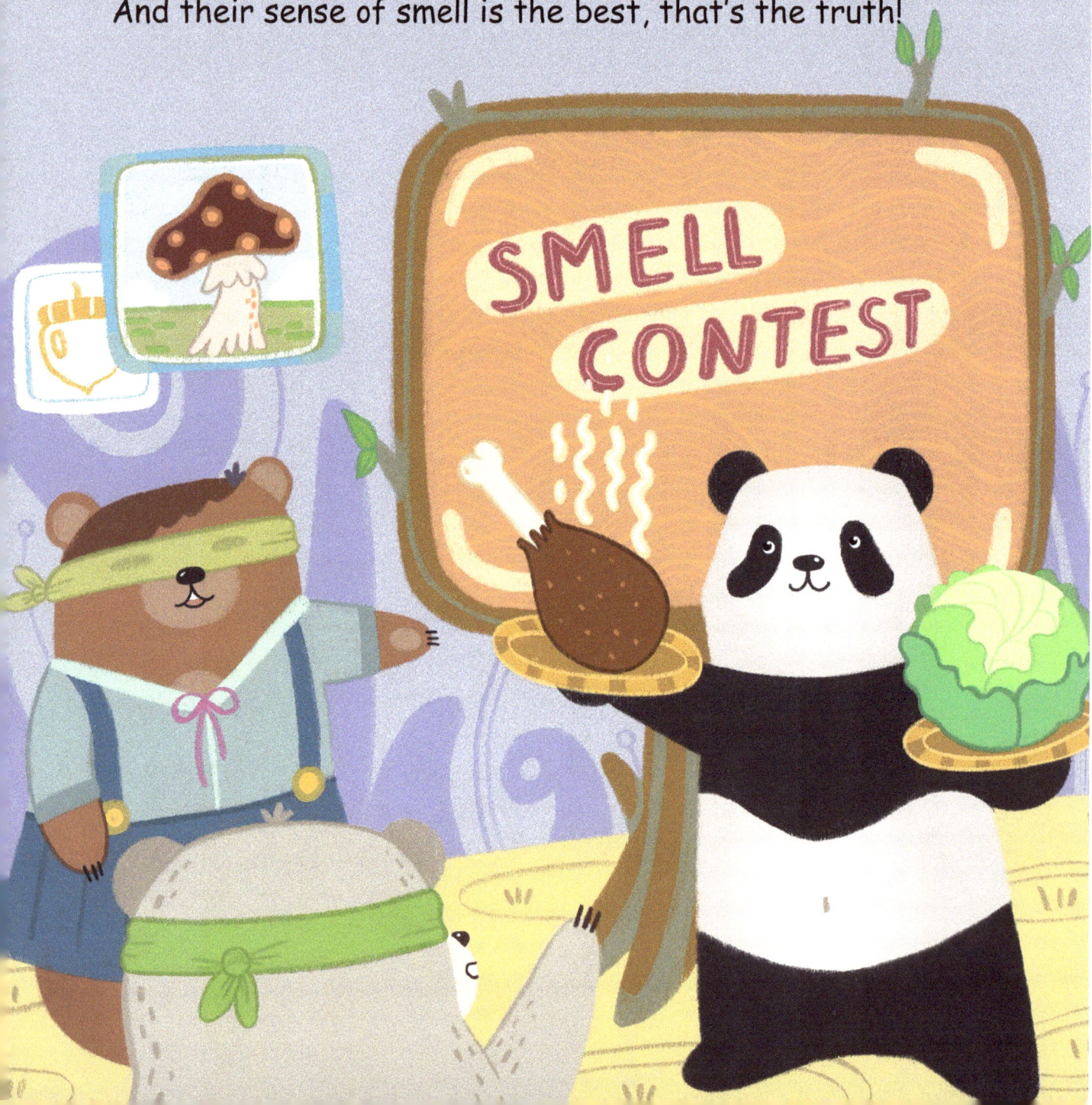

A male bear is a boar and a female is a sow,
They are smart, fast, and can walk
on their back legs somehow.

Cute sloth bears, live in hot,
steamy jungles - nowhere else at all.
They live in India,
Sri Lanka and Nepal.

They sleep in caves but don't hibernate -
There's no snow where sloths live,
so a long winter nap is not their fate.

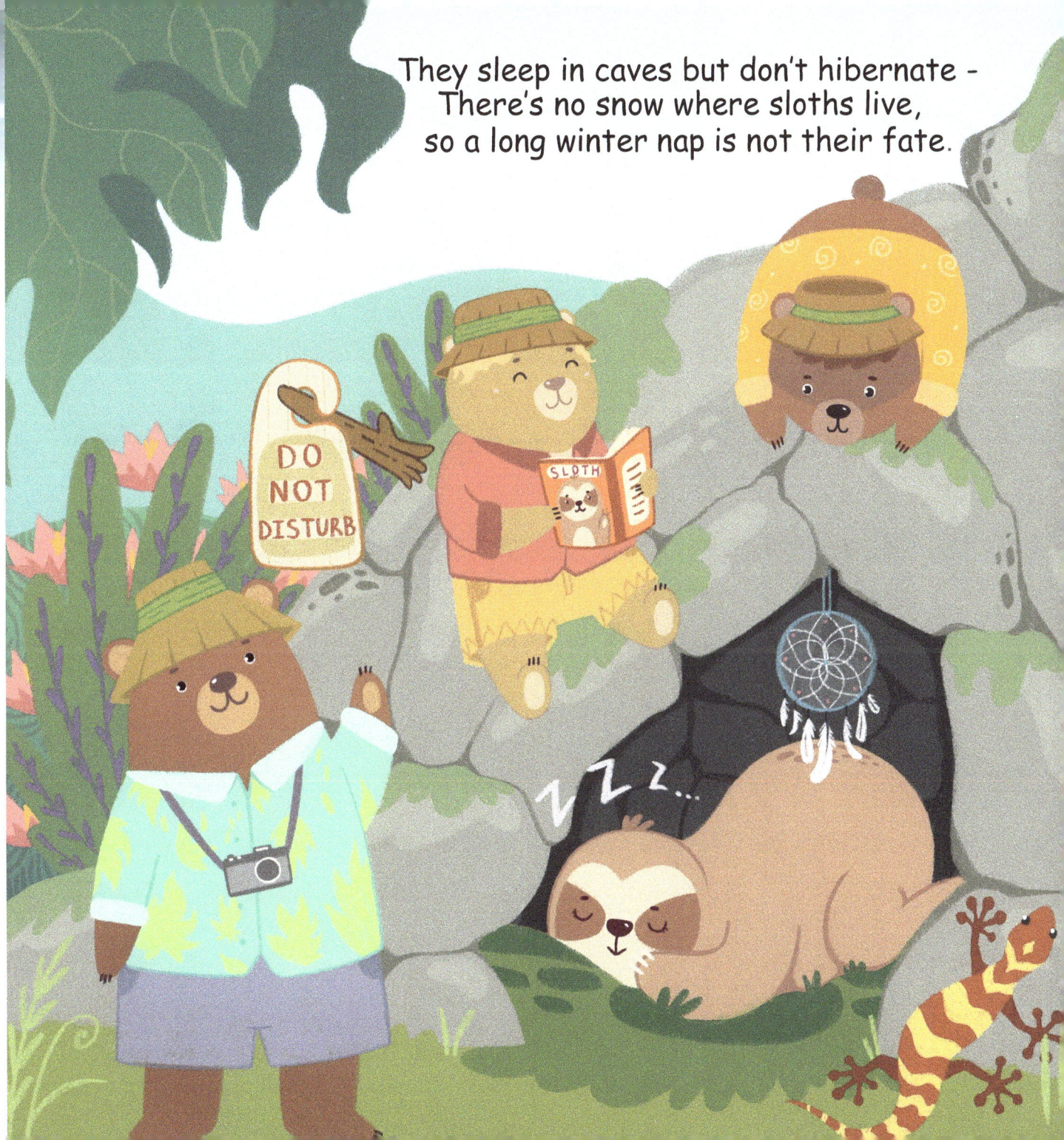

To find the Speckled Bear, also
known as the Andean bear,
Look at a map of Southern American
and you'll find it there.

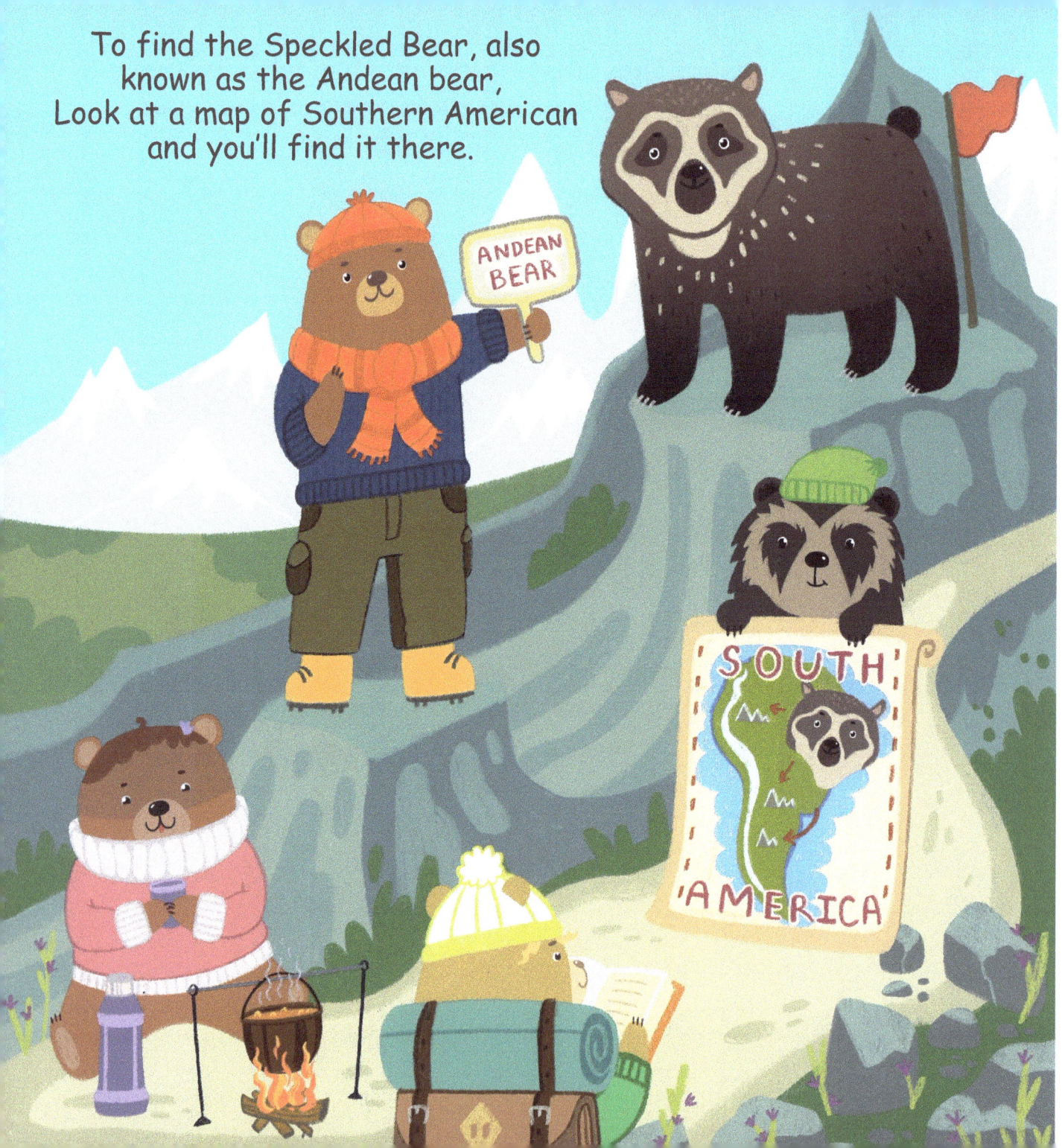

The Asian black bear is often called the
Moon Bear and that name's right
Because on its chest is a white
V-shape, bright as the moon light.

MOON
BEAR

ASIAN
BEARS

There is a bear that lives where icy winds blow.
It's Mr. Polar Bear, who lives in the snow.

POLAR
BEAR

It's hard to believe his skin is really all black,
His see-through hair looks white on his back.

A polar bears' world is snow-fall white,
As he floats on icebergs throughout the night.

He blends in well in his world that's so ice cold,
Polars are the largest of bear with a bite that is bold.

Grizzlies are other big, brown bears that we know.
They are huge and dangerous –
so be careful where you go.

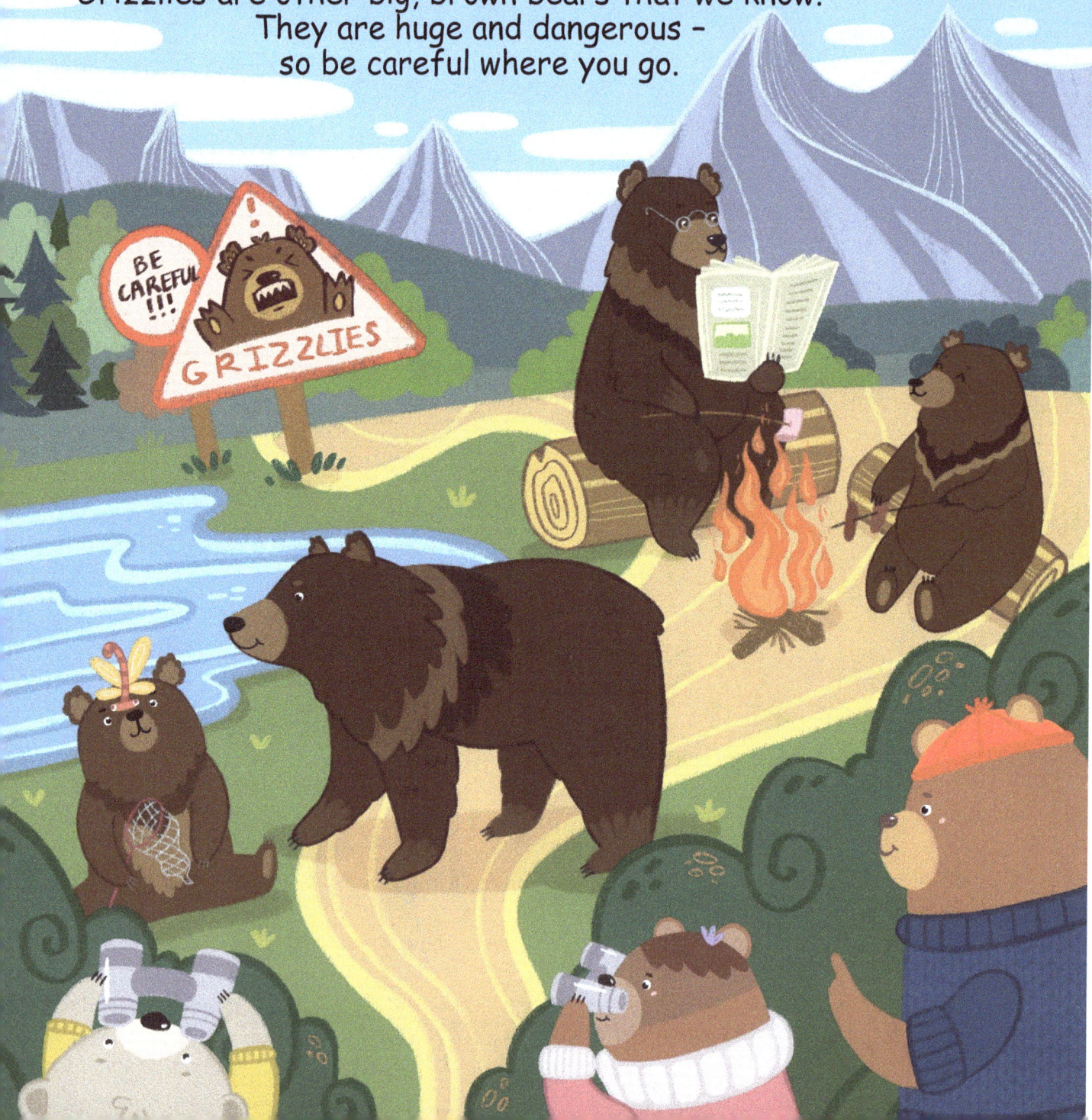

They can be up to seven feet tall when they stand. Grizzlies eat a lot – they are at top of the food chain – which for them is grand!

The Sun Bear is the most miniature bear of all,
But its ten-inch tongue is rather long for a bear so small.

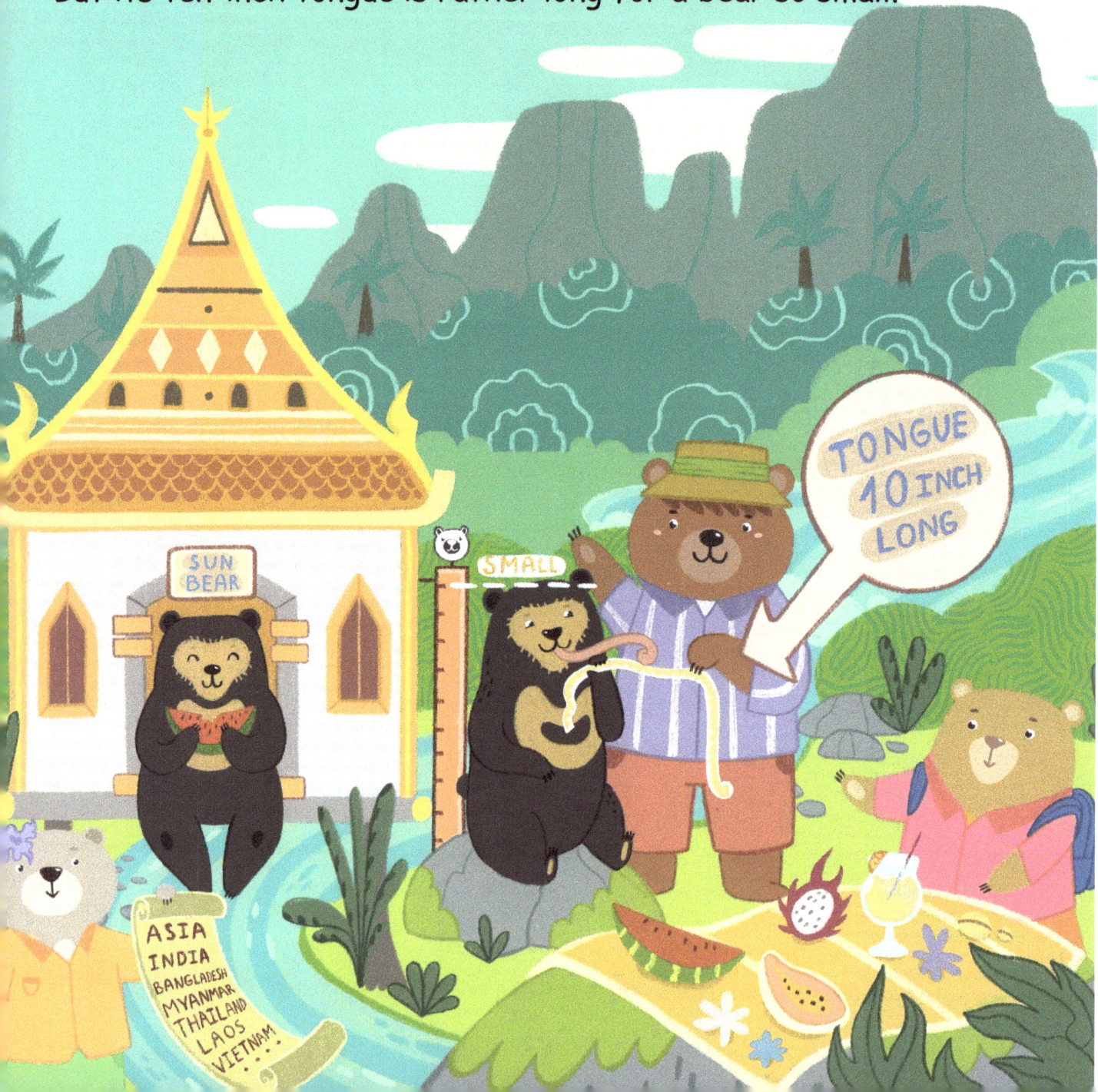

AMERICAN
BLACK
BEARS

American black bears live in Canada,
North America, and Mexico.
Their strong claws make them expert
tree climbers - up they go.

CANADA

AMERICA

MEXICO

Bears don't fully hibernate, they
just don't drink and eat.
They take long, long winter naps then
stretch their legs and feet.

STRETCH

DON'T HIBERNATE

DON'T EAT & DRINK

Bears, don't like to leave
their warm cosy dens, I bet.
But, a grumpy bear wakes up to
leave when things get too wet.

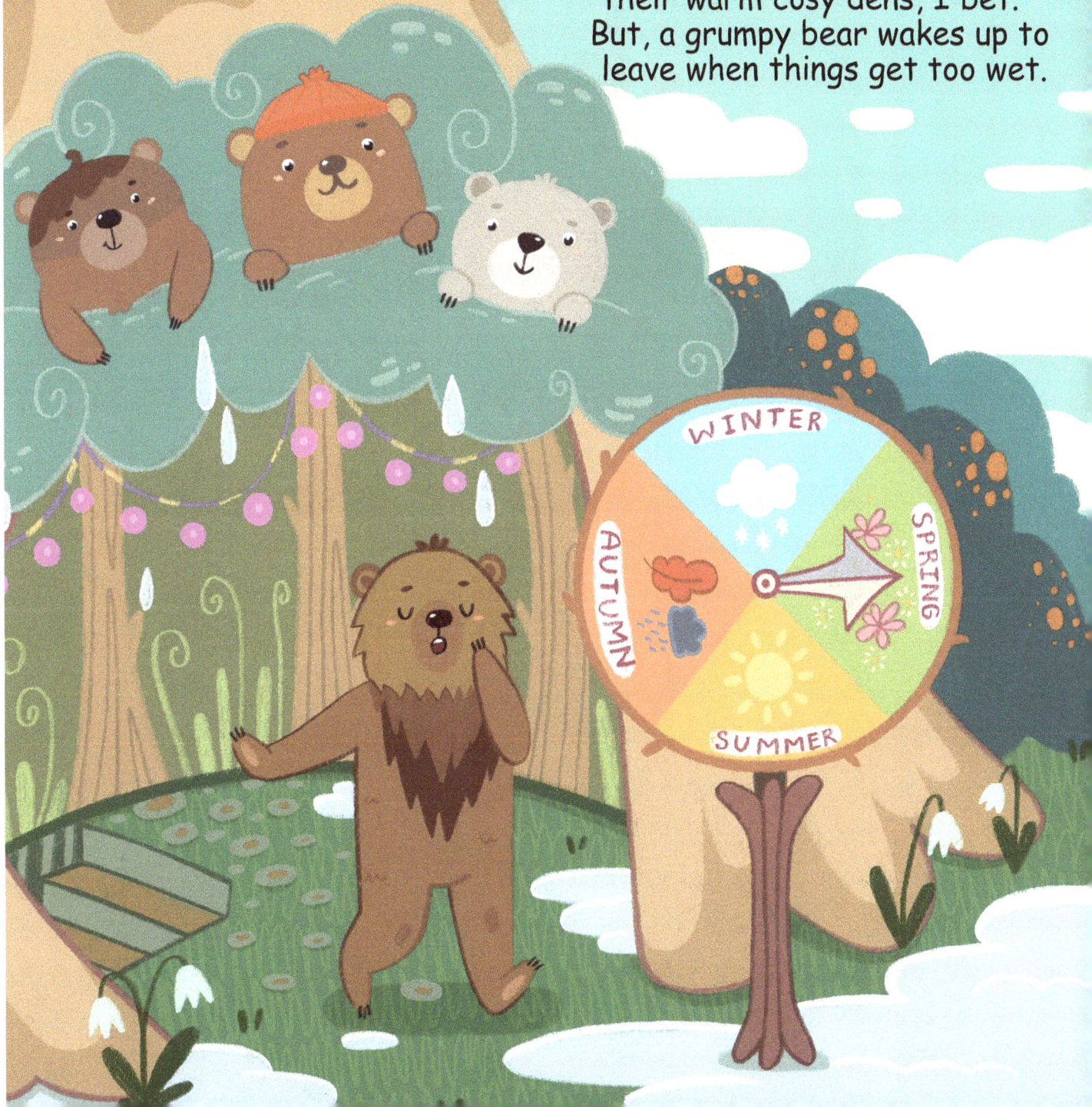

One day, a greedy brown bear put
both arms around a tree.
He was so strong he brought
it down and ate the honey!

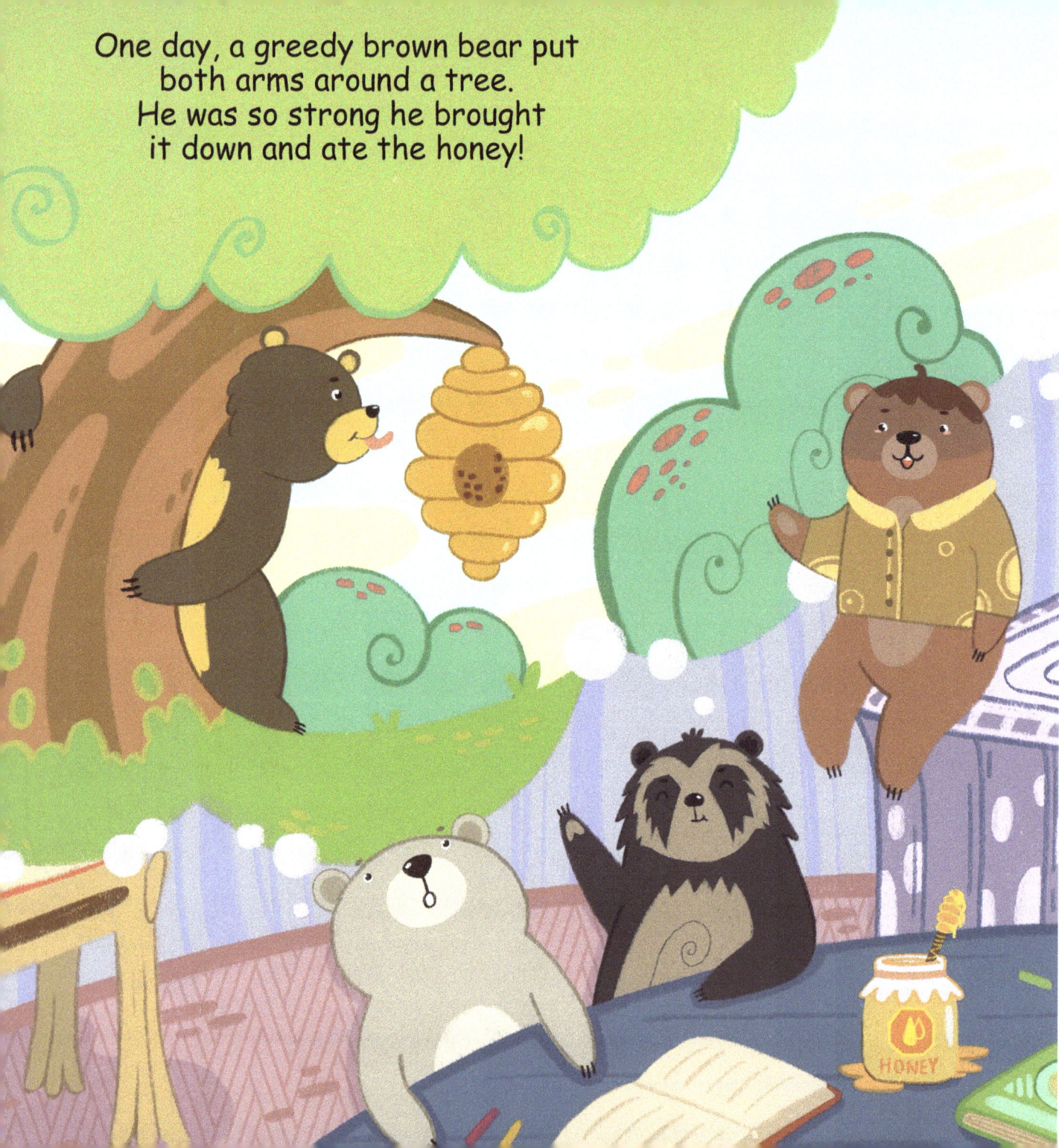

As he put his tongue in and slurped,
you could hear the bees complain.
So he let the tree snap back
upright into the sky once again!

Buzz..

Buzz..

Buzz..

JAM

Berries, nuts, insects and fish are what bears love to eat,
And, yes, like Pooh, they often also love a honey treat!

POOH

HONEY

It would be so bear-able if bears were in charge,
With their meals so sweet and the portions so large!

The End

Fun Facts About Bears :

Bears are animals that are very smart. They have a fantastic ability to find their way around in the world and their skills to do this are better than people's ability to find their way around. Although bears are well-known animals, the following facts may surprise you about these magnificent creatures:

•Bears have large brains compared to their body size

•Bears use tools for play or hunting

•Bears have excellent senses of hearing, smell, and seeing. They can smell food miles away and see fruit on bushes very far away as well

•Bears care deeply about families and are very sad when one of the family members are lost

•Baby bears are called cubs

•Bear cubs are very playful

•Bear cubs moan and cry if they are separated from their mommies

•Some bears that live in Asia make their nests in trees to have their cubs

•Some people honor the bear and consider them a symbol of strength, power, and love

•There are eight different types of bears and they are scattered across the globe: polar bears, giant pandas, sun bears, sloth bears, spectacled bears, brown bears, Asian black bears, and North American black bears

•Bears range in size. Sun bears are the smallest with most adults only reaching at 4 feet tall and 60 pounds. Polar bears are the largest with some becoming very large at 10 feet tall and 1,700 pounds

More Fun Facts about Bears :

- Bears live about 25 years in the wild, but can live 50 years in zoos where they are fed well and protected
- Male bears are called 'boars'
- Female bears are called 'sows'
- Bears 'hibernate' in the winter when food is not available for them. Hibernating is sleeping and they live off their body fat during this time
- While hibernating, mommy bears can have as many as 4 baby cubs. They are without hair and need their mommies for warmth and food
- Bear cubs stay with their mommies for 1 1/2 to three years
- Baby bears learn everything from their mommies
- Most bears live alone and travel alone
- Some bears have a gap in their front teeth so they can such termites and ants easily
- Bears walk on all 4 legs, but they are able to walk on their back legs
- Bears have very large paws and very big claws
- A group of bears is called a 'sloth' of bears - which means 'slow' but bears can run as fast as 40 miles per hour
- Most bears are active at night time
- Panda bears ARE bears
- Pandas are highly regarded in Asian countries
- Panda only eat bamboo and have a digit on their paws like a thumb
- Pandas can do handstands to leave their scent on trees
- Koalas are NOT bears

David R Morgan lives in England. He is a talented full-time teacher and writer.

He has written music journalism, poetry and children's books. His books for children include : 'The Strange Case of William Whipper -Snapper', three 'Info Rider' books for Collins and 'Blooming Cats' which won the Acorn Award and was animated for television. He has also written a Horrible Histories biography : 'Spilling The Beans On Boudicca' and stories for Children's anthologies.

For the last 5 years he has been working on his Soundings Project with his son Toby, performing his own poetry/writing to Toby's original music. This work is on YouTube, Spotify and Soundcloud.

Other Books by David R. Morgan

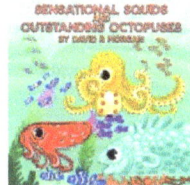

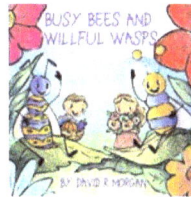

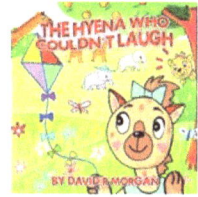

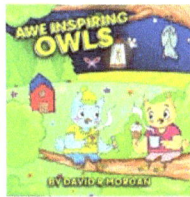

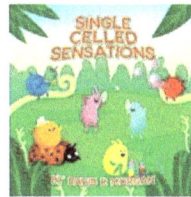

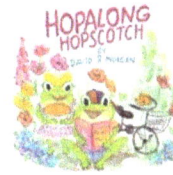

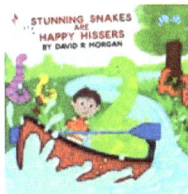

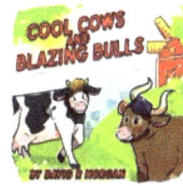

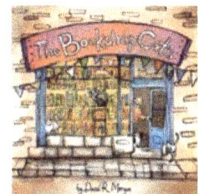

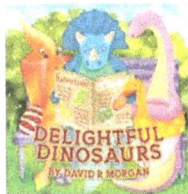

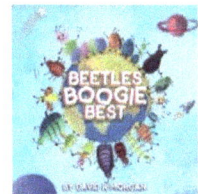

Ants are fANTastic

SENSATIONAL SOUNDS OF OUTSTANDING OCTOPUSES BY DAVID R MORGAN

BUSY BEES AND WILLFUL WASPS BY DAVID R MORGAN

SNAILS AND SLUGS SLIMY SUPERSTARS BY DAVID R MORGAN

THE HYENA WHO COULDN'T LAUGH BY DAVID R MORGAN

AWE INSPIRING OWLS BY DAVID R MORGAN

Wonderful Whirling Whining Worms

SINGLE CELLED SENSATIONS

HOPALONG HOPSCOTCH

Butterfly Beauties and Magical Moths

STUNNING SNAKES ARE HAPPY HISSERS BY DAVID R MORGAN

Turtles and Tortoises are Tremendous!

COOL COWS AND BLAZING BULLS BY DAVID R MORGAN

FABULOUS FROGS AND TERRIFIC TOADS

The Bookshop Cafe

DELIGHTFUL DINOSAURS BY DAVID R MORGAN

BEAUTIFYING BELLS

RUNAWAY RAGTIME

CRABS ARE CRAB ABLE

BEETLES BOOGIE BEST

And many more to come!

More Books by David R. Morgan

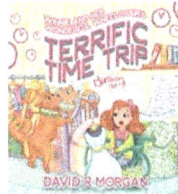

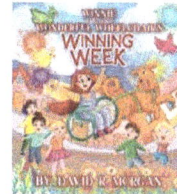

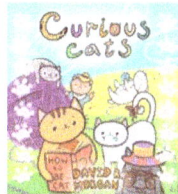

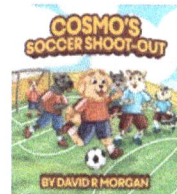

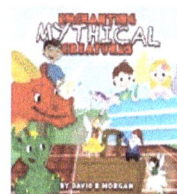

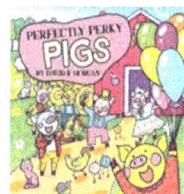

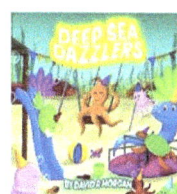

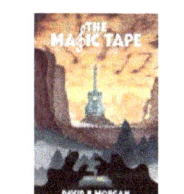

And many more to come!

www.ingramcontent.com/pod-product-compliance
Lightning Source LLC
Chambersburg PA
CBHW042333030426
42335CB00027B/3324